MARVELS and MYSTERIES

The world is full of stories about strange, mysterious monsters.

Most monsters don't really exist. We like them because they m...

...the terrifying Jersey Devil, live only in...

(or perhaps because of)...children...

...particular...and then

...finding we are safe. It's fun to believe in monsters sometime...

MONSTERS

Paul Mason

Smart Apple Media

This edition first published in 2005 in the United States of America by Smart Apple Media.

Smart Apple Media
1980 Lookout Drive
North Mankato
Minnesota 56003

First published in 2005 by
MACMILLAN EDUCATION AUSTRALIA PTY LTY
627 Chapel Street, South Yarra, Australia 3141

Visit our website at www.macmillan.com.au

Associated companies and representatives throughout the world.

Copyright © Paul Mason 2005

Library of Congress Cataloging-in-Publication Data

Mason, Paul, 1967-
    Monsters / by Paul Mason.
    p. cm. – (Marvels and mysteries)
    Includes index.

    ISBN 1-58340-774-X

    1. Monsters — Juvenile literature. I. Title.   J
    GR825.M223 2005   o o i. 994
    001.994 dc22   mas
                                                          2005042864

Edited by Vanessa Lanaway
Text and cover design by Karen Young
Page layout by Karen Young
Illustrations by Jacqui Grantford
Maps by Karen Young
Photo research by Jes Senbergs

Printed in China

Acknowledgments
The author and the publisher are grateful to the following for permission to reproduce copyright material:

Front cover photograph: Mokele-Mbembe, courtesy of Fortean Picture Library/William M. Rebsamen.

Texture used in cover and pages, courtesy of Photodisc.

Aquarius Photo Library, pp. 15, 16; Coo-ee Historical Picture Library, pp. 5, 11, 28; Corbis, pp. 7, 8, 9, 21, 27; Fortean Picture Library, p. 23; Fortean Picture Library/Rene Dahinden, p. 22; Fortean Picture Library/William M. Rebsamen, p. 24; Fortean Picture Library/ John Sibbick & Fortean Times, p. 4; Fortean Picture Library/Richard Svensson, p. 20; Fortean Picture Library/Anthony Wallis, p. 19; Kobal, pp. 10, 12, 14; By permission of the National Library of Australia, p. 29; Photodisc, p. 17; Photolibrary.com, pp. 13, 26.

CONTENTS

GLOSSARY WORDS

When a word is printed in **bold**, you can look up its meaning in the glossary words box, and on page 31.

TIME

Some of the stories in this book talk about things that happened a long time ago, even more than 2,000 years ago. To understand this, people measure time in years Before the Common Era (BCE) and during the Common Era (CE). It looks like this on a timeline:

2000   1500   1000   500   0   500   1000   1500   2000   2500

Years BCE   **Years CE**

It's a WEIRD WORLD

The world is full of stories about strange, mysterious monsters. Some, like the terrifying Jersey Devil, live only in a particular place. Others, like **vampires**, appear in tales from all around the world.

Are monsters real?

Most monsters don't really exist. We like them because they make a good story (or perhaps because they help scare naughty children into behaving!). Something inside most of us enjoys being scared and then finding we are safe. It's fun to believe in monsters sometimes, even though we know there's no such thing.

LOCATION FILE

Location: Pines Barrens, New Jersey, U.S.
Creature: Jersey Devil
Date: 1735 onward
Description: Legendary creature about 4 feet (1.2 m) tall, with a huge head like a horse's, sharp yellow teeth, and small wings.
Activities: Stamps about on roofs scaring people, eats livestock, and perhaps small children.

Descriptions of the Jersey Devil make it sound very like *chupacabras*, the "Goatsucker" (shown here). This legendary creature is reported in Latin American countries.

DIRE
JAME

The search for weird creatures

Some weird creatures are **controversial**. Lots of people think that a monster lives at the bottom of Loch Ness in Scotland. Others are convinced that Bigfoot stalks the woods of North America. Some people spend a lot of time trying to prove that these creatures (and others) exist.

Top five movie monsters

There are lots of weird creatures in movies. Here are some of them:

- Dracula, a vampire
- Godzilla, a giant dinosaur-like monster
- King Kong, an enormous gorilla
- Zombies, dead bodies brought back to life
- Frankenstein's monster, who was made of parts of dead bodies.

GLOSSARY WORDS

vampires   made-up people who have died, yet continue to "live" by drinking the blood of the living

controversial   causing discussion and disagreement

Legendary MONSTERS

Ancient legends told tales of some incredible animals. According to these legends, travel was a dangerous business. Visitors to distant lands could expect to meet a variety of terrifying and mysterious creatures, whether they went by sea or by land.

Giants

Almost all the world's people tell stories of giants. Giants are often said to be fierce, violent creatures. Today, scientists know of a condition called gigantism. Gigantism can cause people to grow up to 9 feet (2.7 m) tall. Perhaps it was people suffering from gigantism who first inspired stories of giants.

····· The Gryphon was a legendary flying monster. Half eagle and half lion, it was eight times the size of a true lion. The gryphon's favorite snack? Human flesh.

The Manticore

It would be very bad luck to meet a Manticore on your travels. This fierce beast had a head like a man and a lion's body. The Manticore's tail was a bit like a scorpion's, and could fire poisonous darts at its victims. Fortunately, there is no evidence that Manticores ever really existed!

Ancient Greek monsters

Cyclops – Giants with one large eye. In Greek legend, three Cyclopes made thunderbolts for the leader of the Gods, Zeus.

Medusa – one of the three Gorgons. The Gorgons were creatures with snakes for hair. They were so ugly that anyone who looked at them turned to stone.

Pegasus – an **immortal** winged horse.

Chimera – a fire-breathing monster with the head of a lion, the body of a goat, and the tail of a serpent.

Pegasus, the immortal winged horse, was said to be the offspring of Medusa and Poseidon, God of horses and the sea.

GLOSSARY WORDS

immortal   living forever

Monsters of the seas

Old sailors' stories told of dangerous creatures that waited in the depths of the sea. Some threatened violence against any ship they met. Others lured sailors to their deaths through trickery.

Mermaids and Sirens

Mermaids would **enchant** sailors with their beauty and their singing. When the sailor came near, the mermaid would put her cap on his head and take him down under the waves to live with her. Sirens were **mythical** creatures with beautiful voices. Any sailor who heard them was drawn to his death on the rocks nearby.

Odysseus was said to be the only man ever to have heard the Sirens' song and survived.

Odysseus and the Sirens

When the Greek hero Odysseus had to sail past the Sirens, he blocked his sailors' ears with wax. That way they could not hear the song and be tempted on to the rocks. The sailors tied Odysseus to the mast, so that he heard the song but could not be drawn away by it.

MINI FACT

Descriptions of the Sirens differ. Some people said they were birds with the heads of women. Others said they were women with wings and bird legs.

Sea serpents

Sea serpents are giant sea snakes. Legends say that they used to attack ships. Creatures similar to sea serpents, called *Tylosaurus*, lived in the oceans when dinosaurs walked the Earth. *Tylosaurus* had giant jaws and grew to 60 feet (18 m) long. Even today, the oceans are home to eel-like creatures called oarfish. Oarfish can grow up to 40 feet (12 m) long.

Old stories of giant squid attacking boats may be true. In 1930 the Norwegian tanker *Brunswick* was attacked three times in one day by a giant squid. The creature tried to wrap its arms around the ship. The third attack ended when the squid was hurt by the propeller.

FACT FILE

Giant squid

Giant squid used to be accused of attacking the boats of explorers and travelers. This may not be true, but the squid do exist.

- Giant squid grow up to 60 feet (18 m) long.

- Their eight arms and two tentacles are covered in grippy suckers. These are used to drag prey into the squid's beak-like mouth.

GLOSSARY WORDS

enchant — to hypnotize or fill with joy

mythical — made up or part of an ancient story

WEREWOLVES

Location: Western and Central Europe
Date: from about 400 BCE

Werewolves are imaginary creatures who can turn themselves from human to wolf form. As wolves, the werewolves go on rampages, biting and killing their victims. Anyone they bite becomes a werewolf too.

Stories of werewolves have existed for thousands of years. In Europe they first became widely feared during the 1500s and 1600s. At that time people thought werewolves were the helpers of the Devil. Anyone convicted of being a werewolf was burned alive as punishment.

Werewolf hallucinations

Some researchers have suggested that werewolf sightings in the Middle Ages were caused by drugs, because:

- at the time, most poor people ate rye bread

- rye bread sometimes contains a fungus called ergot

- ergot causes people to **hallucinate**. It may have led them to think they saw werewolves, or even that they were werewolves.

In movies, werewolves turn from human to wolf when there is a **full moon**. Often they are unable to control the change, and do not remember the terrible crimes they have committed while in wolf form.

LOCATION FILE

Location: Zacatecas, Mexico

Name: The Aceves family

The Aceves family live in Zacatecas. They have become famous because of the hair that grows all over their bodies, including their faces. Because of a rare **genetic** condition, the family members look like the werewolves seen in films.

◁···· These people are not werewolves. The hair all over their bodies and faces is caused by a genetic condition.

Werewolf origins

Where did the idea of werewolves come from? In the past, wolves were a real danger to people. Scientists now know of a rare condition that makes humans look like movie werewolves. Perhaps these two things helped to produce the idea of the werewolf.

MINI FACT

Between 1520 and 1630 there were over 30,000 werewolf trials in France alone. Thousands of people died a horrible death by burning as punishment after being convicted of being a werewolf.

GLOSSARY WORDS

hallucinate	to imagine something is happening when it is not
full moon	when the moon is at its brightest and most circular
genetic	physical characteristics passed on from parent to child

Haitian ZOMBIES

Location: Haiti
Date: from about 1530, when African slaves were first brought to Haiti

Zombies are people who are said to have died and been brought back to life. They have no **will** of their own, and are forced to serve the person who woke them from death.

Zombies are part of voodoo beliefs. Voodoo is a common religion in Haiti, a Caribbean country near Cuba and Jamaica. People there believe that sorcerers are able to create zombies, raising the dead to act as their slaves. Each year, graves are dug up and people say that the bodies have been taken as zombies.

Zombies at the movies

Zombies have been popular characters in horror movies since the 1930s.

- The famous horror actor Bela Lugosi starred in a movie called *White Zombie* in 1932.

- The horror classic *Night of the Living Dead* (1968) features flesh-eating zombies, woken from death by radiation from a crashed satellite.

- In 1979 the follow-up, *Dawn of the Dead*, also featured flesh-eating zombies.

 In the movie *Night of the Living Dead*, anyone bitten by one of the flesh-eating zombies became a zombie themselves.

Do zombies really exist?

Scientists working in Haiti have found that voodoo "sorcerers" use a special potion to create zombies. It includes the poisons of a particular toad, plus the deadly **pufferfish**. When a person is given the potion, it slows their heartbeat and breathing so much that they seem to have died. The person is buried, then dug up and revived by the sorcerer. More drugs keep them zombie-like.

There are about 100 different kinds of pufferfish. Many carry a poison that can **paralyze** any living thing. The poison is about a thousand times more deadly than cyanide. It is one of the ingredients in Haitian zombie potions.

GLOSSARY WORDS

will   the ability to think and make decisions for yourself

pufferfish   a poisonous fish that can puff itself up to look big

paralyze   make unable to move

VAMPIRES

Vampires are mythical creatures who are sometimes called the "undead." This is because they are said to be humans who have died and come back to life. They then survive by drinking the blood of other living things.

The best-known vampire of all is Count Dracula. A writer named Bram Stoker invented Dracula in 1897. In Stoker's book, Dracula is the first, original vampire. Most modern vampire stories are based on *Dracula*.

PEOPLE FILE

Name: Vlad Tepes

Born: 1431

Died: 1476

Nicknames: Vlad Dracula (which means "son of the dragon" or "son of the Devil"), and Vlad the Impaler.

Famous for: Vlad Tepes was the ruler of Wallachia (now part of Romania) famed for his bloodthirsty cruelty.

Vlad Tepes was one of the inspirations for Bram Stoker's character "Dracula." Vlad was known as "Vlad the Impaler" because he often impaled his enemies on wooden stakes. On St Bartholomew's Day in 1459, he impaled 30,000 people from the city of Brasov, then feasted among the dead and dying.

Vampire characteristics

According to legends, all vampires have similar characteristics. They must sleep in the soil of their homeland. Their powers are weak in daylight—some stories say vampires are destroyed if exposed to sunlight. They can change their shape. Vampires are said to find it difficult to cross water. Most of all, to survive they must drink the blood of living things .

 Stories say that any person bitten by a vampire will become one when they die.

GLOSSARY WORDS

impaled   pierced through with a sharp, pointed object

15

Could vampires exist?

Between about 1600 and 1800 in Europe, many people looked for proof that vampires existed. Many graves were dug up so the bodies could be examined for evidence. Scientists can now explain the "evidence" that was found:

"Evidence" Hair and beard had grown on a dead body.

Explanation Scientists now know that skin shrinks back after death, making it seem as though hair has grown.

"Evidence" The body's old skin had peeled off, leaving fresh skin underneath.

Explanation This is called "skin slippage." The outer layer of skin peels away, leaving the inner layer visible.

"Evidence" The old nails had fallen off and new ones had grown.

Explanation Nails do fall off dead bodies. The "new ones" were probably the hardened skin beneath the old nail.

"Evidence" The body had fresh blood in its mouth.

Explanation This was not fresh blood but a result of the body starting to rot.

••••➤ The bodies of suspected vampires used to have stakes driven through their hearts to "kill" them. People thought the body cried out as it "died." In fact the noise was made by gases escaping as the stake was hammered down.

Vampires around the world

Stories of vampires exist in many regions of the world. These are just a few.

- **Aswang** (Philippines) – a beautiful woman by day, Aswang becomes a flying **fiend** by night.

- **Asanbosam** (West Africa) – a vampire who lives in dark forests, lying in wait for unwary travelers at night.

- **Kuang-shi** (China) – a terrifying-looking vampire said to be able to fly.

- **Loogaroo** (Caribbean) – every night, Loogaroo removes its skin at a "Devil Tree," before flying off in search of victims.

- **Tlaciques** (Mexico) – a strange vampire, which can turn itself into either a ball of flame or a turkey.

Tlaciques. a vampire from Mexico, could turn itself into a turkey in order to disguise itself from its victims.

GLOSSARY WORDS

fiend   an evil being

17

MYSTERIOUS ape-men

For hundreds of years, sightings of mysterious ape-men have been reported all around the world. They appear all over, from the forests of North America to the wooded hills of Australia. Photos and films are said to show the ape-men. But no proof that they exist has ever been uncovered.

What do the ape-men look like?

Stories say the ape-men have the body of an ape, but walk on their back legs. In many stories they have a face more like a man's than an ape's. Usually the ape-men are shy and avoid contact with people. Most are said to be human-sized or larger.

Canada
Sasquatch

Caucasus Mountains
Almas

China
Gin-Sung and Tok

Himalayan Mountains
Yeti

USA
Bigfoot

East Africa
Mau

Japan
Higabon

Brazil
Mapinguary

Australia
Yowie

Zaire
Kikomba

New Zealand
Maero

FACT FILE

Ape-men sizes

Ape-men come in three different sizes:

Size	Ape-man	Example
3–4.5 feet (1–1.5 m) tall	Dwarf	the Higabon from Japan
4.5–6 feet (1.5–2 m) tall	Man-sized	the Almas of the Caucasus
6–15 feet (2–5 m) tall	Giant	the Tok from China

What could the ape-men be?

Two main explanations have been put forward for the ape-men. The first is that they are some kind of very shy, clever ape, only rarely seen. The second is that the giant ape-men are the last surviving relatives of *Gigantopithecus*. This was a huge creature that scientists think died out 500,000 years ago.

FACT FILE

Australia's ape-man

Australia's ape-man is usually called the Yowie. It has been known of for hundreds of years, since long before the arrival of the First Fleet in 1788.

- The Yowie is most often reported in coastal New South Wales and Queensland.

- It is said to be bigger and more powerful than a man, and covered in hair.

MINI FACT

The Almas are ape-men believed to live in the remote Caucasus Mountains of Kazakhstan. One story says that in the mid-1800s, one was captured and lived among humans. She had six human children, and her descendants may still live in the region today.

The Himalayan Yeti

The most famous ape-man of all is the Yeti. No one knows for sure what the Yeti is. But several reliable witnesses have reported seeing it in the snows of the Himalayan Mountains.

The Yeti is also known as the "**Abominable Snowman**," because of its fearful behavior. Ancient stories from Nepal tell of gangs of Yetis terrorizing whole villages. They are said to have been very common on the mountain slopes near Mount Everest. If Yetis still exist today, they are very rare.

Location: Himalayan Mountains
Date: first sighting unknown

Yetis are said to be between 4.5 and 6 feet (1.5–2 m) tall and very powerful. They are covered in fur and have a pointy-topped head.

FACT FILE

What is the Yeti?

Evidence suggests that the Yeti could actually be some sort of ape.

- A section of skull said to belong to a Yeti has orange-colored hair like an **orangutan**'s.

- The isolated valleys of the Himalayas could be home to large apes.

- Yetis seen in the mountains could be lone males moving to new territory.

Has anyone ever met a Yeti?

Many people say they have seen Yetis. A mountaineer, Sen Tensing, was walking home one night when he and his friends met a Yeti coming the other way. Tensing hid behind a boulder, shaking with fear and hardly daring to breathe. Finally the Yeti moved back down the path the way it had come.

This photo is said to show Yeti footprints. People have claimed to see Yeti footprints that were 12 inches (30 cm) long and eight inches (20 cm) wide.

PEOPLE FILE

Name: Tensing Norgay (1914–1986)

From: Nepal

Description: Tensing was (with New Zealander Sir Edmund Hillary) the first to climb Mount Everest, in 1953.

Famous for: On their climb, Tensing and Hillary reported seeing mysterious footprints in the snow, like those of the Yeti.

GLOSSARY WORDS

abominable — very unpleasant or disagreeable

orangutan — a large ape that lives in Borneo and Sumatra

21

Bigfoot

Bigfoot is a mysterious giant creature that is said to live in the woods of North America. It is sometimes called Sasquatch. Bigfoot's name comes from its giant-sized feet. One footprint measured 18 inches (45 cm) long by seven inches (18 cm) wide.

When was Bigfoot first seen?

Native American people have known of Bigfoot for hundreds of years. However, the first written records come from much later. One of the first reports was in 1811, when a Canadian trader traveling near Jasper, Alberta, found footprints in the snow measuring 14 inches (35 cm) long by eight inches (20 cm) wide.

FACT FILE

Cousins of Bigfoot

Creatures like Bigfoot have been reported in lots of different places:

- In Florida, the **Skunk Ape** apparently gets its name from its appalling smell.

- The **Wookie**, from Louisiana, may have given the *Star Wars* character its name.

- In California, the **Oh-mah** is said to haunt the forests.

This photo is said to show the Skunk Ape, in Sarasota County, Florida.

Is there any evidence Bigfoot exists?

The best evidence that Bigfoot could exist is a film shot in 1967 by two people on a Bigfoot-hunting expedition. They claim to have spotted a female Bigfoot near a river. The men caught only a few moments of footage before their film ran out. No one has ever been able to prove that the film is a fake.

This is a shot from a famous "Bigfoot movie" shot in 1967. Some people have claimed that the blurry film shows someone dressed in a gorilla suit, rather than Bigfoot.

FACT FILE

Tall tales

The Reverend Elkanah Walker lived with the Spokane people in northwest America.

- In 1840 Walker reported that the Spokane believed giants lived in the mountains.

- The giants left footprints 1.5 feet (0.5 m) long.

Freshwater MONSTERS

For hundreds of years, the deep, dark waters of the world's lakes have been thought to contain terrifying monsters. Many of the monsters look like plesiosaurs, water creatures that were common when dinosaurs stalked the Earth. Some people claim that the lake monsters are descendants of the plesiosaurs. No one has ever found any proof these monsters exist, though.

Mokele-Mbembe

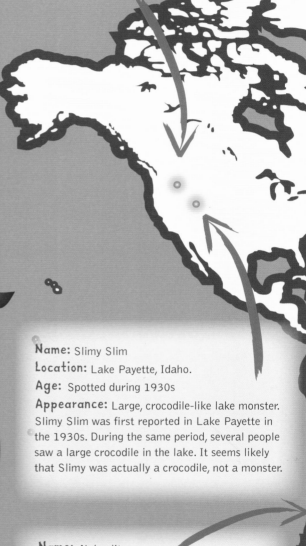

Name: Ogopogo (*Nantiaka* to Native Americans)
Location: Lake Okanagan, Canada
Age: Uncertain—first spotted by Native Americans hundreds of years ago.
Appearance: Large, serpent-like monster.
Ogopogo features in a song written in 1926:
*"His mother was an earwig,
His father was a whale,
A little bit of head and hardly any tail—
And Ogopogo was his name."*

Name: Slimy Slim
Location: Lake Payette, Idaho.
Age: Spotted during 1930s
Appearance: Large, crocodile-like lake monster. Slimy Slim was first reported in Lake Payette in the 1930s. During the same period, several people saw a large crocodile in the lake. It seems likely that Slimy was actually a crocodile, not a monster.

Name: Nahuelito
Location: Lake Nahuel Huapi, Argentina
Age: Uncertain—first reported 1890s.
Appearance: Large, serpent-like monster. Sightings of Nahuelito have been made since the 1890s. Some stories, though, still claim that the monster was created by nuclear tests done nearby in the 1960s!

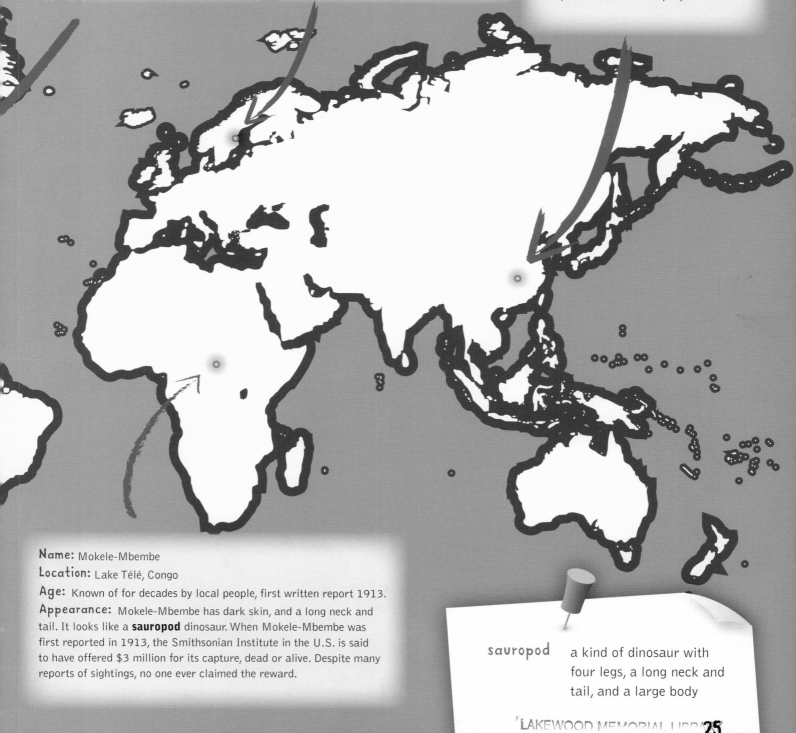

Name: Champ
Location: Lake Champlain, U.S./Canada
Age: First reported 1600s
Appearance: 10–30 feet (3–10 m) long, with a thin body, long neck, and flat head. Champ, the monster from Lake Champlain, is described as looking similar to plesiosaurs, which lived during the age of the dinosaurs.

Name: Storsjoodjuret
Location: Lake Storsjon, Sweden
Age: First spotted in the 1600s.
Appearance: 13–43 feet (4–15 m) long, with an eel-like body, long neck, and flat head. Lake Storsjon is said to be home to more than one monster. But several monster-hunting expeditions have failed to find any evidence that they exist.

Name: Unnamed
Location: Lake Tianchi, China
Age: recent reports from 2002 and 2003
Appearance: A black monster with a horse-like head. Rumors of a monster of some sort in Lake Tianchi have been around since 1903. Then, reports said that a creature like a huge buffalo had leaped from the lake, let out a terrifying roar, and attacked three people.

Name: Mokele-Mbembe
Location: Lake Télé, Congo
Age: Known of for decades by local people, first written report 1913.
Appearance: Mokele-Mbembe has dark skin, and a long neck and tail. It looks like a **sauropod** dinosaur. When Mokele-Mbembe was first reported in 1913, the Smithsonian Institute in the U.S. is said to have offered $3 million for its capture, dead or alive. Despite many reports of sightings, no one ever claimed the reward.

sauropod   a kind of dinosaur with four legs, a long neck and tail, and a large body

25

The Loch Ness MONSTER

Location: Loch Ness, Scotland
Date: from 1933

The Loch Ness Monster is the most famous lake monster of all. Thousands of tourists visit the loch (lake) each year, hoping to see "Nessie." Despite many attempts, no one has ever managed to prove that Nessie exists.

Nessie is usually said to be about 30 feet (10 m) long, with a 6-foot (2-m) neck, a small head, and a long tail. She was first reported in 1933. Reports said an enormous creature had been seen "rolling and plunging" in the water. A **craze** of Nessie sightings began. People even claimed the monster had been seen crossing the road!

This photo was taken by Colonel Robert Wilson and Christian Spurling in 1934. For years people were convinced that it showed the Loch Ness monster. In 1993, Spurling admitted it was a fake.

more. possibly They eat

Living giant Amph[i]
compared with an ext[...]
(Drawn to Scale).

L. R. Brightwell.

Ten feet.

[a]ll fish and crayfish, and though able
[...]nove quickly on occasion could
[...]ly put up the motor-launch spe[ed]
[...]ed to the "monster," far [...]
with a sheep,
[am]phibians [...]

The first reported Loch Ness sighting says that St Columba rescued a swimmer from a hungry lake monster that had entered the River Ness. This picture was printed in the *Daily Mail* in the 1930s, after another sighting was reported.

Since the 1930s, many people have tried to prove that Nessie exists. In April 1960, a man called Tim Dinsdale filmed an object moving across the loch. Then in 1972 underwater photographs seemed to show something in the water. One researcher detected a large creature moving beneath his boat using **sonar**. But no one has ever proved that Nessie exists.

LOCATION FILE

Location: Scotland

Name: Loch Ness

Loch Ness would be an excellent place for a monster to hide.

- It is the largest freshwater lake in Britain.

- It is 24 miles (38 km) long and 1.5 miles (2.4 km) wide at its widest point.

- In some places the loch is more than 1,000 feet (300 m) deep.

GLOSSARY WORDS

craze   a short-lived, strong interest in something

sonar   a way of detecting objects under water, using sound waves

The BUNYIP

Location: Australia
Date: first sighting unknown

The Bunyip is a legendary creature from Australia. It is said to live in the swamps, creeks, and billabongs. According to Aboriginal stories, the Bunyip is a fearsome killer to be avoided at all costs.

What does the Bunyip look like?

No one knows for sure what the Bunyip looks like. In Aboriginal stories it sometimes has feathers, or scales like a crocodile. It can also appear with flippers, walrus-like tusks, and a horse's tail.

Non-Aboriginal stories describe two different Bunyips. One has a dog-like face and a shaggy coat. The other has a shaggy coat and a long neck. These Bunyips are far less dangerous than the original kind.

The Bunyip appears in many Aboriginal stories. He has a lot of different shapes, but is always dangerous to the people who live nearby.

28

Is there any evidence that the Bunyip exists?

The only real evidence that the Bunyip might exist was found in 1846. An unusual skull was discovered in New South Wales. Scientists could not identify it, and stories quickly spread that it was a Bunyip skull. The biggest mystery is that the skull itself soon disappeared, and has never been seen since!

Fiery Creek, Victoria

The Challicum Bunyip

The local Aboriginal people believed that a Bunyip died at Fiery Creek, near Challicum Station in Victoria, countless years ago.

• They marked the outline of the body with spears, and cleared the grass away where the Bunyip had died.

• The site was still there when white settlers arrived in 1840. Over the years, though, it has disappeared.

FACT FILE

MONSTER gallery

The Hydra

DOES NOT EXIST

Location: Greece

Date: not known

Description: A multi-headed monster that lived in Lake Lerna. One head was immortal. The others grew back if they were cut off. The Hydra was finally killed by the Greek hero Hercules. He cut off its heads and sealed them with fire. Then Hercules cut off the immortal head and buried it beneath a rock.

The Loch Ness Monster

NO EVIDENCE DISCOVERED

Location: Loch Ness, Scotland

Date: first reported 1933 CE

Description: A long-necked, dinosaur-like monster that has been attracting tourists to Loch Ness for almost 100 years.

Zombies

DO NOT EXIST

Location: Haiti

Date: from mid 1500s

Description: A zombie is a person who has died and been brought back to life to serve their "zombie master."

Bigfoot

EVIDENCE DISCOVERED

Location: North American woodlands

Date: not known

Description: A giant, ape-like creature that walks on its back legs like a man. The cousins and other relatives of Bigfoot have been reported in forests around the world.

The Yeti

NO EVIDENCE DISCOVERED

Location: Himalayan Mountains

Date: not known

Description: The ape-man of the Himalayas has been frightening local people for centuries. Once said to be common, it is now only rarely reported.

The Bunyip

NO EVIDENCE DISCOVERED

Location: Australia

Date: not known

Description: water-dwelling monster with various different appearances. Feared by Aborigines for thousands of years, the Bunyip is one of the few Aboriginal mythical creatures to be reported by non-Aboriginal Australians.

Werewolves

DO NOT EXIST

Location: All around the world

Date: descriptions from 400 BCE

Description: A human who transforms into a wolf or wolf-like creature when the Moon is full.

Vampires

DO NOT EXIST

Location: all around the world, but especially the Balkan Mountains

Date: not known

Description: Vampires are said to be dead humans who rise again to drink the blood of the living.

GLOSSARY

abominable something that is very unpleasant or disagreeable

controversial something that causes discussion and disagreement

craze a short-lived, strong interest in something

enchant to hypnotize or fill with joy

fiend an evil being

full moon when the moon is at its brightest and most circular

genetic physical characteristics passed on from parent to child

hallucinate to imagine something is happening when it is not

immortal living forever

impaled pierced through with a sharp, pointed object

mythical made up or part of an ancient story

orangutan a large ape that lives in Borneo and Sumatra

paralyze make unable to move

pufferfish a kind of poisonous fish that can puff itself up to look big

sauropod a kind of dinosaur with four legs, a long neck and tail, and a large body

sonar a way of detecting objects under water, using sound waves

vampire made-up people who have died, yet continue to "live" by drinking the blood of the living

will the ability to think and make decisions for yourself

INDEX